THE BUBBLE OF CONFIRMATION BIAS

Alex Acks

Enslow Publishing
101 W. 23rd Street
Suite 240
New York, NY 10011
USA
enslow.com

Published in 2019 by Enslow Publishing, LLC.
101 W. 23rd Street, Suite 240, New York, NY 10011

Library of Congress Cataloging-in-Publication Data

Names: Acks, Alex, author.
Title: The bubble of confirmation bias / Alex Acks.
Description: New York : Enslow Publishing, [2019] | Series: Critical thinking about digital media | Includes bibliographical references and index. | Audience: Grades 7-12.
Identifiers: LCCN 2018015225| ISBN 9781978504714 (library bound) | ISBN 9781978505667 (pbk.)
Subjects: LCSH: Social media—Psychological aspects—Juvenile literature. | Prejudices—Juvenile literature. | Belief and doubt—Juvenile literature. | Disinformation—Juvenile literature.
Classification: LCC HM742 .A299 2018 | DDC 302.23/1—dc23
LC record available at https://lccn.loc.gov/2018015225

Printed in the United States of America

To Our Readers: We have done our best to make sure all websites in this book were active and appropriate when we went to press. However, the author and the publisher have no control over and assume no liability for the material available on those websites or on any websites they may link to. Any comments or suggestions can be sent by email to customerservice@enslow.com.

CONTENTS

INTRODUCTION

"**M**en always leave the toilet seat up." This is probably a truism you've heard, particularly if you live in a mixed-gender household. Women tend to state it as a fact, for which they can reel off incidents they clearly remember of when this has happened. Men protest that they do so put the toilet seat down, and if they forget, it's certainly not often enough to warrant this accusation. Both sides of the Great Toilet Seat Position War are absolutely convinced that they're right.

On its face, the entire thing is funny. It's a favorite joke comedians of any gender can reach for if they want an easy laugh. But it's also a prime example of a quirk of human thinking that plays a major role in all of our lives and profoundly (and often negatively!) affects our understanding of the world around us: confirmation bias.

Confirmation bias is the tendency of people to interpret, remember, and specifically seek out information that confirms beliefs they already have. This means that when new information confirms someone's beliefs—or prejudices—they tend to embrace it. On the other hand, when new information challenges something a person believes, they tend to want to

Between ten and twenty-five million people believe that the 1969 moon landing was a hoax. It was, however, not; you can see the flagpoles planted in modern satellite imagery.

reject it. Confirmation bias is also called "myside bias" because of the way people look only for information that supports their side.

Confirmation bias affects our everyday lives in a multitude of ways, from the obvious to the subtle. You've probably heard of conspiracy theories before—for example, there's a group of people who believe that humans haven't actually landed on the moon. (A surprisingly large group of people believe this, between ten and twenty-five million, according to Phil Plait, who writes about the "Moon Landing Hoax" in his book *Bad Astronomy*.[1]) Confirmation bias is a big part of the building and persistence of these conspiracy theories. The people who believe in them seek out information that confirms their conspiracy theory ("You can't see the stars in the astronaut photos!") and reject any information that contradicts their belief ("I don't believe that the photos all had very short exposure times and the stars were too faint because it was daytime on the moon!").

While this kind of thing can seem funny when it's people claiming we didn't land on the moon, it can become a lot more harmful when confirmation bias helps people spread the false claim that vaccines cause autism (they don't[2]) or the vicious lie that the Sandy Hook school shooting was a hoax.[3] Confirmation bias in the public has made debating and acting on important issues such as global climate change extremely difficult. Climate change "skepticism" can be confirmed by things as simple as local record high and low temperatures, with people in countries that have had a lot of recent record low temperatures more skeptical that climate change is real.[4]

No one is immune to confirmation bias. It's just part of how the human mind works. But being aware of its existence and how it can creep into your life is the best defense. A growing feeder of confirmation bias in the modern world is the internet, particularly social media, where it's easy to surround yourself with a "bubble" of like-minded people. In this text we will explore the ways the social media bubble encourages confirmation bias—and how to combat it.

1

A Brief History of Confirmation Bias

A Nameless but Very Annoying Phenomenon

The first historical mention we have of something that sounds a lot like confirmation bias is by the Greek historian Thucydides, who lived from 460–395 BCE. In *The History of the Peloponnesian War*, he wrote: "… for it is a habit of mankind to entrust to careless hope what they long for, and to use sovereign reason to thrust aside what they do not fancy."[1] Ibn Khaldun, an Arab historian who lived from 1332–1406, noted in the Muqaddimah: "…if the soul is infected with partisanship for a particular opinion or sect, it accepts without a moment's hesitation the information that is agreeable to it."[2]

Similar mentions were made by Dante Alighieri in *The Divine Comedy*, Francis Bacon in *Novum Organum*, and philosopher Arthur Schopenhauer in *The World as Will and Representation*. The Russian novelist Leo Tolstoy even mentions it in *The Kingdom of God Is Within You*: "The most difficult subjects can be explained to the most slow-witted man if he has not formed any idea of them already; but the simplest thing cannot be made clear to the most intelligent man if he is firmly persuaded that he knows already, without a shadow of a doubt, what is laid before him" (translated by Constance Garnett).[3]

It's fair to say that it's been a truth long-understood that people become entrenched in their beliefs and biases, and tend to deny information that challenges their position. But as a recognized psychological effect, it still lacked definition.

Wason's Research

Confirmation bias was given a name by the English psychologist Peter Wason, in 1960. He conducted an experiment to research the effect, involving subjects trying to identify and apply a rule to sets of three numbers.

At the beginning of the experiment, the participants were told that one set of numbers (2, 4, 6) fit the rule. Then they were asked to generate their own sets of numbers, which the person running the experiment would

Dante is cautioned by St. Thomas Aquinas in *The Divine Comedy* that "opinion—hasty—often can incline to the wrong side, and then affection for one's own opinion binds, confines the mind."

confirm or deny worked with the rule as well. The real rule for the experiment was just "any ascending sequence"—so any set of three numbers that went from smallest to largest. But the participants in the experiment kept focusing on much more specific rules that they hypothesized, and then only giving sequences of numbers to the experimenter that would fit the rule they'd made up for themselves. For example, a participant might decide that the rule was "even numbers only, each number two greater than its predecessor." So they would only present sets of numbers that validated that very specific hypothesis to the experimenter (like "14, 16, 18" and "30, 32, 34") and have those confirmed, so they became even more convinced that they'd figured out the rule.

Wason interpreted his results as the participants showing a preference for confirmation over what is called "falsification." Falsification is an important concept in science; it is the process of disproving a hypothesis or theory. In fact, for a hypothesis to be tested, it must be falsifiable, meaning it must be something that could be proven false with the appropriate test results. For the participants to shy away from testing sets of numbers that could falsify their hypothesized rule seemed to indicate a desire to not be challenged or proven wrong.[4, 5, 6, 7]

Klayman and Ha

Joshua Klayman and Young-Won Ha disagreed with Wason that his experiment showed confirmation bias as we have come to understand it. Because of Wason's experimental design, Klayman and Ha analyzed the results as showing more of a tendency for the participants to make up tests that were consistent with their hypothesis. The distinction is subtle but important: where Wason saw a wider sign of cognitive bias at work, Klayman and Ha saw a shortcut that people use in reasoning. It's an imperfect shortcut, and definitely not one consistent with scientific testing, but Wason wasn't testing scientists either.

A different version of Wason's experiment that asked participants to figure out more specific rules rather than the broad one Wason had started with supported Klayman and Ha's analysis.[8] This type of experiment began to focus more on the way people tested hypotheses, leaving the idea of "confirmation bias" behind. To try to locate "true" confirmation bias, a different experiment design was needed.

Stanford Experiments

In the 1970s, researchers at Stanford began designing less abstract experiments to see if confirmation bias was a real effect. In one experiment, conducted in 1975 by Ross, Lepper, and Hubbard, the researchers showed a group of undergraduate volunteer pairs of different suicide notes. The subjects of the experiment were told that one of the notes in the pair was a genuine suicide note, and the other had been made up. Then they were asked to identify which of the notes was real, and which was a fake. Some of the subjects were told that they guessed almost every note correctly, and some were told that they consistently failed. The purpose of the experiment wasn't to test their detective skills—it was to see how they'd react to being given false positives and negatives. The experimenters then told the students that they'd been deceived to some extent

Types of Confirmation Bias

Biased information search: Looking only and specifically for information that supports what you already think. For example, when you write an essay, do you only go looking for things that directly support what you're planning to say?

Biased interpretation of data: People can and do interpret the same information differently—and in ways that already support what you believe. A good example is how people interpret evidence related to global climate change depending on what they want or believe to be true.

Biased memory: There is even a tendency to remember things that reinforce a belief you have. This is the kind of confirmation bias at work with the toilet seat example from the introduction.

about how right or wrong they'd been—and then were asked to estimate how many "hits" or "misses" they thought they'd gotten.

The results of the self-estimation were curious. Students who had been given a lot of false positives tended to still estimate their "hits" at higher than average—and those who had been given false negatives tended to estimate their "misses" at higher than the real average. A belief in their abilities, given falsely, persisted even after the lie was revealed.[9]

Confirmation bias is the tendency of people to interpret, remember, and specifically seek out information that confirms beliefs they already have.

A few years later, Lepper, Ross, and Anderson conducted more experiments; they gave student volunteers packets of information with fake biographies for a firefighter and fake results for a "Risky-Conservative Choice Test." Half the students got one version (we'll call it "Version A"), which showed the firefighter as playing it safe and indicated he was very good at his job. In the other version ("Version B"), the firefighter was still shown as always taking the safe option on the test, but was said to be very bad at his job. The experimenters then revealed that their firefighter was entirely fictitious, but they asked the students to describe their own beliefs—would a successful firefighter always aim for the safer option? Students who got Version A said that a good firefighter would avoid risk; students who got Version B said a good firefighter would take risks. Even knowing the firefighter was completely made up, they seemed to base their opinions off the poor information they'd been given.[10]

Confirmation bias (and its related effects) was shown to be real and very pernicious.

Do video games cause real-world aggression in players? Those who already believe this also readily believed fake studies that showed that very outcome.

Continuing Experiments

The Stanford experiments weren't the last word on biased thinking, even if they were the start of it. Modern psychological research continues to look at the myriad of ways cognitive bias effects our thinking. A study by Greitemeyer in 2014 examined how different groups of people would react to studies about how violent video games affect (or don't) the people who play them.

Participants read two fictitious studies about video game violence affecting player aggression, one which showed no effect and one which showed there was effect. Sadly (and now unsurprisingly), those who believe violent video games increase aggression evaluated the fake study that supported their beliefs more highly than the fake study that showed no effect—and vice versa for their opposites. The study as a whole showed that new information led both sides to become more certain of their views.[11]

This effect is something you can easily observe in your daily life as well—just look at how different people react to new scientific studies about global climate change.

Social Media Algorithms and Confirmation Bias

Rise of the Algorithmically Sorted Timeline

When most of the major social media sites started— Facebook, Twitter, Instagram—users viewed their feeds in some form of chronological order. A user would see the posts of everyone that they followed, put in the order in which they were posted, though it depended on the site if it would be oldest or newest posts first.

Starting in 2011, Facebook began to sort its feed using algorithms[1] intended to show users the most "interesting" posts at the top of their feeds. An "algorithm" is a set of rules to follow; in this case, it was a new set of rules for the computer program that determined the order Facebook posts would be displayed in.

Twitter followed suit in 2016, Instagram in 2017,[2] and even Snapchat began an algorithm-based redesign of its site at the end of 2017.[3] The sites generally claim that this algorithmic sorting is beneficial to users, who often miss the vast majority of feeds on their posts because they follow more users than they can keep up with, so they will see a snapshot of the most compelling and interesting content at the top of their feed. This has also been viewed by users as a way for the various social media sites to push sponsored or advertising posts, making it more difficult for smaller businesses to reach their followers.[4]

An algorithm is a list of rules that describe how a task will be performed. They can also control what you see on social media platforms.

Some sites do allow the sorting algorithms to be turned on and off. Currently, Facebook allows algorithmic sorting to be turned off temporarily, while Twitter allows users to turn it off permanently. Sites like Instagram and Snapchat don't allow any user control of how they view their timeline.

Other sites, like YouTube, are structurally dependent on their sorting and recommendation algorithms; users can't turn them off or directly affect them at all. Engineers for YouTube have described its algorithms as one of "the largest scale and most sophisticated industrial recommendation systems in existence."[5]

YouTube has always depended on algorithmic recommendations for its users, and algorithms set the "up next" autoplay videos for the site.[6]

How Algorithms Work

An algorithm is a list of rules that describe how a task will be performed. People use algorithms all the time, for jobs and school, and even in our regular lives. We just don't tend to call them algorithms. For example, if you want to get a candy bar, then there are multiple algorithms you could use to decide how to get a candy bar.

You never see all the steps it takes data to reach its goal—but it can be like running an obstacle course. Sometimes the algorithm helps; sometimes it diverts you from the true goal.

Vending Machine Algorithm
1. Go to vending machine.
2. Put in quarters.
3. Input number of candy bar you want.

Convenience Store Algorithm
1. Go to convenience store.
2. Go to candy aisle.
3. Pick out candy bar.
4. Pay.

Computers use algorithms all the time as well. If a computer program is a set of step-by-step commands that tell the computer what you want it to do, the algorithm is the list of rules that tells the computer how you want it to accomplish that task. For a social media site, the "program" says "show users an activity feed." The algorithm is the set of rules that determines how the feed is set up.

We don't know exactly what the algorithms by Facebook, Twitter, Instagram, YouTube, or other social media sites are, because they are proprietary to their platforms. We only have a general sense of how they are constructed, from what the companies have been willing to tell tech reporters. Facebook told reporters at Slate that their algorithms try to predict what its users will like using hundreds of factors to produce a "relevancy" score. Factors include elements such as "likes," the amount of times people spent looking at a post, number of shares, and many other factors. The relevancy score of a post then determines what order the posts show up on the feed, with the highest scores at the top. Facebook also seeks feedback from people regarding the quality of what's shown on feeds in order to keep tweaking the algorithm.[7] Twitter told Slate that its algorithm has focused on showing popular tweets, and the tweets of people a user interacts with often first.[8]

Ultimately, this means that the rules used to determine what is seen on social media sites are not created by the users. Rather they are designed by human programmers, and as such will reflect what the person or team (or company) thinks is relevant, which may not be the same as what the user thinks is relevant.[9] Despite the common perception that algorithms are somehow impartial because they're being run by machines, it's important to remember who created the algorithms (people), and why. Recent research has shown that the construction of algorithms and the results they produce can reflect the subconscious biases of their creators—including racism.[10] In one example, an algorithm that was supposed assess how likely it was that a defendant would commit a crime again in the future falsely marked black defendants at twice the rate it did white defendants.[11]

If algorithms can and do reflect the bias of their creators, can they also reflect the biases of their users?

The Algorithmic Bubble

The focus of social media algorithms is effectively to show a user more of what they already like; this is a situation that invites and strengthens confirmation bias in subtle ways. A 2016 study by Del Vicario, et al. in the *Proceedings of the National Academy of Sciences of the United States of America (PNAS)* that looked at the spread of conspiracy theories on Facebook found that "selective exposure" was a major driving force—that people already interested in conspiracy theories looked at, were shown, and spread posts that supported their conspiracy theory. Social media tended to "homogenize" and "polarize" groups of users.[12]

Considering how the algorithms previously discussed work, it makes sense. The algorithms show people posts that are popular and similar to ones they have liked or engaged with before. Users tend to like and share things that they agree with, care about, and think are important.[13] The algorithms will

"Diversity is good. Pass it down."

An echo chamber is a closed system where similar beliefs and opinions reverberate but do not change. Diversity is awesome—so why is everyone at the table still a white male?

show them more posts that are similar to the ones they already agreed with and liked. As pointed out by Slate, prioritizing the posts of people users agree with and interact with often may very well have the unintended side-effect of insulating them from other viewpoints.[14]

Of the types of confirmation bias discussed previously, this effect is most closely related to biased information search. But it's more subtle and pernicious than that. In a biased information search, a person actively seeks out information that agrees with what they already believe. On social media, the algorithms are now doing all the work—they will show users posts that they will probably like and agree with, without the user needing to make any effort to bypass what could challenge their beliefs. In fact, the user might never know that posts they disagree with are out there.

This effect is more commonly called an echo chamber. In reality, an echo chamber is an enclosed space created to allow sounds to reverberate; if you stood in one and shouted your opinion about something, your own voice would just bounce back to you. On social media, the echo chamber is the enclosed social space created by who users choose to follow and what posts are read, which often "echoes" back and amplifies beliefs and opinions that are the same as their own.

CREATING YOUR OWN BIAS BUBBLE

Muting, Blocking, and Self-Isolation

In a 2017 interview with Quartz, Bill Gates said social media "lets you go off with like-minded people, so you're not mixing and sharing and understanding other points of view."[1]

While algorithmic sorting is the most pernicious and subtle way that confirmation bias can come into play on social media, users have always been able to easily create their own echo chambers. Social media sites have muting and blocking (even if they call them different things) features. Blocking normally prevents you from seeing another user's posts, and keeps them from being able to see yours. Muting features can silence other users—or depending on the site, particular terms or hashtags—while still giving them access to your posts.

Both muting and blocking are important moderation tools for use in social media. Muting other users instead of blocking or unfollowing can be useful for things as simple as avoiding social drama or avoiding spoilers for your favorite TV show.[2] Muting can also be psychologically necessary to some users

Muting and blocking social media accounts can be an important part of online strategy to limit drama—but you don't want to limit everything you disagree with because this only deepens your own echo chamber.

by allowing them to avoid subjects or hashtags that they find upsetting or harmful to their mental health. Blocking allows users to escape from abusive behavior or trolls, since particularly on Twitter, reporting accounts for bad behavior hasn't been a guarantee of getting help.[3]

However, these tools can also promote self-isolation on social media sites. There is already a major "selection bias" in who users choose to follow. In science, a "selection bias" indicates that a group of experimental subjects or data to be analyzed has been selected in such a way that

Social media allows you to choose whom you listen to, and it takes special effort to seek out opinions and people with whom we disagree. Challenge yourself!

it's not representative of the population being considered. Of course, who people follow on social media isn't going to be representative of the population around them! Because people can choose who to follow, they will tend to pick people they find interesting or funny, or ones that they know personally (and might feel obligated to follow). Some sites like Facebook offer a "groups" function, which allows users to come together around shared interests—or beliefs. Groups can easily become miniature echo chambers of confirmation bias, as well as giving advertisers stationary targets at which to aim tailored ads.[4]

Because the focus of who you follow on social media is so personal—it's who you're choosing to listen to—it's almost inevitable that it will be people who tend to agree with you. They're the ones saying things that you will most often like and enjoy hearing, after all. It takes special effort and resolve for a user to seek out people with whom they actively disagree—and a desire to be challenged in that way.

This is where mute and block functions can become unhealthy on social media. Users may wield mute and block as a way of avoiding viewpoints or information that challenge their beliefs. For example, if someone on Facebook keeps talking about "Second Amendment rights" while you believe in some form of gun control, it can become extremely frustrating—and it might seem better to not have to look at that stuff at all.

A Pew Research Center poll conducted in 2014 focused on the way people with different political leanings used social media and news sources. It found that people who self-identify as "consistently conservative" were most likely (47 percent) to have like-minded friends on social media, and "consistently liberal" people are most likely (44 percent) to be willing to block others over political disagreements. On average, 23 percent of all people were likely to see posts on Facebook that agreed with their political views, and 26 percent of all people surveyed had blocked or muted others because of their politics.[5] While blocking others can be very satisfying at times, it also means cutting off viewpoints and new information that might not agree with your beliefs.

This plays very heavily into confirmation bias, since people are already primed to avoid data that challenges what they already think. Users on social media can very easily mute or block anyone who disagrees with them, ensuring that they will only ever hear opinions or see posts that agree with what they already think. This can be another kind of biased information search, a way to ensure that the only information you ever see on social media affirms your beliefs, whether those beliefs are about politics or about who had the best album this year.

When Sites Suggest Whom You Should Follow

Instagram and Twitter constantly suggest other accounts a user might be interested in following, while Facebook suggests groups it thinks a user might be interested in joining. Just like now-standard non-chronological feeds, these suggestions are created by algorithms.

According to Facebook, suggested groups are based off of pages you've liked, groups you're already a member of, groups similar to those you're a member of, and groups that are geographically close to you.[6] Many of these factors look at what you've already liked—and suggest something similar.

Following people from different backgrounds can broaden your point of view. Hearing their experiences can enrich your own—much like reading a book puts you in another point of view.

This can play into the confirmation bias echo chamber, because more of what you already like is not going to provide alternate viewpoints or facts.

Some of Twitter's follow suggestions are based off of contacts uploaded from your address book, and recommend "promoted" (paid for advertisement) accounts. But more importantly to a user's confirmation bias, they will suggest accounts based on your own Twitter activity—what you tweet, who you already follow, and who you interact with. Twitter also looks at your activity from other websites that integrate Twitter, like ones with embedded timelines. If you visit lots of Twitter-integrated websites that involve pie, for example, Twitter will recommend you pie-related accounts (Instagram suggests accounts to follow in a similar fashion).[7] This becomes a way for Twitter to, again, show you more of what you already like, while avoiding things it thinks you won't like. While this isn't harmful if you have a pie-making hobby, it becomes a problem with politically-charged issues like global climate change.

Your Data Is a Resource

It's no secret that the large social media companies make their money off advertising, and their users. Data are the resource they're selling to companies who have products to market. But there's potentially an even darker side to what your data can tell companies about you, and it plays on confirmation bias.

The best example of this is the abuse of Facebook by the firm Cambridge Analytica. In 2014, an academic created a personality quiz app for Cambridge Analytica. They then paid a relatively small number of Facebook users (about 320,000) a negligible amount of money to use the app. Because of the way the app was written, which Facebook now says is in breach of their data policies, everyone who used it also gave the app access to the personal data of all of their friends. This ultimately allowed the company to collect profile data on about fifty million users.[8]

Advertisers can target your preferences on social media. Did you like puppy photos? You may get ads for pet stores and pet adoption agencies. Everything you do online has a distinct value.

Troll Identification

How do you tell if someone is trying to troll you? Sometimes, to paraphrase Supreme Court Justice Potter Stewart, you just know them when you see them. Other trolls are more subtle. Trolls are there to upset you, annoy you, or at the very least, waste your time. Definite troll signs include:

1. Deliberately trying to provoke you or get an emotional response. This can range from concern trolling to outright insults.
2. A sense of entitlement to your time, like demands for response.
3. Use of hyperbole.
4. Personal attacks.
5. Bad spelling and grammar, and weird, nonsensical abbreviations or acronyms.
6. Use of the caps lock.
7. Use of anonymity, in email addresses, user names, or even proxies.

What was this data going to be used for? The ultimate aim was to create predictive psychological profiles with user data, and then use those profiles to specifically target political advertisements at groups of users.[9, 10]   These kinds of advertisements could be tailor-made to play on the effect of confirmation bias, telling specific users just what they would be most likely to believe that could manipulate them in the way the advertisers wanted (in this case, the Brexit and Trump campaigns).[11]

The actual effectiveness of Cambridge Analytica's technique has been called into question by data scientists and psychologists, but it may only be a matter of time before another unethical data firm tries something similar.[12,13] Being able to target advertisements that will appeal directly to someone's psychology would be incredibly useful for any company— and as we've seen, people like being told what they already believe.

Disagreement, Trolling, and Abuse

Even if you don't control your feed thanks to algorithms, you do control who you follow and who can see your account. If you want to avoid feeding your own confirmation bias, it's healthy to follow people and read posts that you disagree with. Sometimes disagreement can be upsetting, but it's important to not confuse simple disagreement with trolling or abuse. If someone on social media is deliberately trying to hurt you, they definitely deserve to be blocked—and to have their account reported.

News, "Fake News," and Confirmation Bias

As more people get at least some of their news on social media, it's important to start considering the effect of two things: our own confirmation bias and how that relates to the proliferation of "fake news."

News and "Fake News" on Social Media

News stories are frequently shared on social media by its users, though some services (Facebook, Reddit, and Twitter) tend to be used more for news than others (YouTube, Snapchat, and Instagram). A 2017 Pew Research Poll found that "two-thirds (67 percent) of Americans report that they get at least some of their news on social media; 78 percent of Americans younger than fifty use social media to get news stories; and over half (55 percent) of those older than fifty do now.[1] News sharing is big on social media, and the trend seems to be that it's only going to get bigger as time goes on.

What Is Fake News?

The term "fake news" became popularized during the 2016 Presidential election due to its use by then-candidate Donald Trump and media figures such as conservative Fox News host Sean Hannity, as a means to discredit news stories detrimental to Trump's campaign or unflattering to him.[2] Merriam-Webster's blog noted in 2016 that, "Fake news is frequently used to describe a political story which is seen as damaging to an agency, entity, or person," though it is by no means always

The rise of news sharing on social media platforms is huge—but too much can overwhelm. Two-thirds of Americans report that they got some of their news from social media.

restricted to politics. It indicates the spread of a spurious or untrue story that purports to be factual. The term is about one hundred twenty five years old.[3]

The spread of false news stories is much older than the use of the term "fake news." One of the earliest known examples is of the Egyptian pharaoh Ramses II spreading the story that the Battle of Kadesh was a major victory for Egypt with Ramses himself playing a prominent heroic role—when in fact the battle was a stalemate.[4] It's safe to say that as long as there has been "news," there have been people spreading "fake news" to further their personal agendas—and probably calling stories they don't like "fake" in order to discredit them.

There is much more detail to discuss about the creation and dissemination of "fake news" in the modern day that goes far beyond our topic of confirmation bias. If you want to know more about "fake news," there's another book in this series that will help you learn more: *Fake News and the Factories that Make It.*

How News and "Fake News" Play into Confirmation Bias

Earlier, we discussed how social media can become an echo chamber, built by selection bias in who you follow and the algorithms that recommend posts. Posts that purport to be somehow factual, like news stories, play even more powerfully into our biases than just hearing the opinions of our friends who agree with us.

People like to believe they are rational actors most of the time. We like to think our decisions and beliefs are backed up by logic, using cold, hard facts. Psychologically, this is often not the case. Most of our decisions get made by fast, intuitive processes in our minds, and there's not necessarily anything wrong with this. If we had to consider everything logically and rationally, we wouldn't be able to react quickly in times of crisis, for example. But an unfortunate side effect of this is that while our logical minds aren't always making the

Fake news has been around a long time; Egyptian pharaoh Ramses II boasted that he won a tremendous battle at Kadesh, immortalizing it on the walls of his temples. Truth is, the battle was a stalemate.

choices, they are very good at rationalizing the decisions after it happens.[5] This is sometimes called post hoc rationalization, meaning rationalization has happened after the fact. Post hoc is often a shortening of the Latin phrase *post hoc ergo propter hoc*, which means "after this, therefore because of this." In this case, the phrase means "after this, rationalization."

This is one of the psychological forces behind confirmation bias. There's an already-existing belief or decision, so our rational brain comes up with the reasoning to justify why it's correct. It seeks out facts and makes arguments that support what's already there—and one of the best ways to line those

One way to eliminate confirmation bias is to slow down the thinking process and logically work through step by step. Start with a question and see where it naturally leads, not where you presume it will go.

facts up is to cherry-pick scientific studies or news stories, depending on what the belief is. The news stories we choose to read, believe, and share are heavily influenced by our biases[6]—and people across the political spectrum have this problem.[7]

On social media, people generally share news stories that they agree with or think are important, which is often deeply entwined with their personal political beliefs. A 2015 study looked at the spread of news stories on Facebook, particularly how much news sharing was "cross-cutting," meaning that it came from or supported a perspective different than that of the user. Three factors were identified in how the news stories were spread:

1. Who a user's friends are (and what news stories they would share);
2. Which news stories were pushed by Facebook's algorithm;
3. Which news stories the user would actually click on (and presumably read).

You'll notice that number two is under the control of Facebook, while factors one and three are controlled entirely by the social media user. The conclusion of the study was that the users had the most power in this equation—they had like-minded friends and were mostly interested in news stories they already politically agreed with. But Facebook's algorithms also had a significant effect. Facebook didn't create the social media echo chamber with its algorithmic feed, but it definitely made it worse.[8, 9]

How does "fake" news fit into this? We've already seen that there can be a problem with social media users focusing on factual news stories (or studies) that they agree with and ignoring the ones they don't. When we're engaging our rational mind and trying to make good decisions, having all of the facts, even ones we don't like, is important. It's best to have the fullest view possible, even if sometimes that makes decisions feel more difficult because we live in a complex world. There are a multitude of examples showing how even with access to all of the facts, people can go off into harmful directions—think about the moon landing hoaxers and anti-vaccination activists who were mentioned in the introduction to this book.

"Fake news" is even more pernicious, because it's non-factual. Often, these made-up stories are specially crafted to tell a particular group exactly what they want to hear, reinforcing those beliefs without even the small amount of ambiguity that comes from the factual world not being black-and-white. "Fake news" stories are often crafted to blur the line between news and entertainment, making them more likely to be shared.[10] How to make posts and stories go "viral" on social media is an area of intense interest and study by psychologists and marketing firms alike[11]—and what has already been learned is easily applied by the creators of "fake news" stories.

Discussion is ongoing as to whether or not "fake news" on social media had a significant influence on the political outcome of the 2016 presidential election. On one side, tech journalists at places like the *Atlantic*,[12] *Motherboard*,[13] and *Wired*,[14] have traced out the psychological influence game of political "fake news." On the other, a meta-analysis—which

No One Is Immune to "Fake News"

In a famous historical example, Sir Arthur Conan Doyle, the creator of the rationalist detective character Sherlock Holmes, was taken in completely by a set of photographs that purported to show fairies interacting with human girls. (These photographs are known as "the Cottingley Fairies.")

Sir Arthur Conan Doyle was a dedicated believer in spiritualism and went to his grave promoting the authenticity of the photographs,[15] despite all evidence that they had been faked using paper cut-outs. Decades after his death, the girls who created the photographs admitted they were fake.[16]

In 2016 and 2017, some journalists were found to be spreading fake negative news about Donald Trump because it spoke to what they wanted to be true rather than what was actually true.[17]

Sir Arthur Conan Doyle was taken in by his own belief that fairies were real. He went to his grave believing the Cottingley Fairy photographs were real.

is a special kind of scientific research that does not run its own experiment, but instead analyzes the results of many other related experiments—found only a "minimal" effect.[18] Nate Silver, who became famous for his accuracy at predicting election results using statistical methods that he honed on baseball, has pointed out that the influence of this "fake news" is difficult to measure because it wasn't a single event.[19] Does "fake news" change anyone's mind, or does it just make those who already believe something untrue even more resistant to realizing their errors? We may never know how large of an influence "fake news" has on our culture as a whole, but we can be wary about what it does to us on a personal level.

It's when something that purports to be fact tells us exactly what we want to hear that is most dangerous. Because "fake news" is often part of targeted campaigns or used to generate profit,[20] from manipulating stock prices [21] to generating advertising revenue from clicks,[22] there's more behind its spread than just users sharing their confirmation bias. There are forces behind the posts that are actively working to see that they are shared more widely.

5

THE SPREAD OF "FAKE NEWS" ON SOCIAL MEDIA

A major question left in the wake of the 2016 presidential election is just how much of an effect the spread of political "fake news" on social media had on the outcome. How does fake news spread on social media—and how much is driven by the sites themselves, versus the users and their confirmation bias?

"Fake News" and Social Media Algorithms

We talked earlier about the three main factors behind the spread of news stories on sites like Facebook. Remember, the factors are: (1) who your friends are, (2) what posts a site's algorithms push, and (3) what posts you choose to look at. The creators of "fake news" already try to influence factor number three by crafting posts that are "clickbait," using outrageous headlines, upsetting pictures, or just an implication that their post is going to tell you exactly what you want to hear. BuzzFeed found that, in 2016, many "hyperpartisan" Facebook pages and news sites were run out of the country Macedonia, often by teenagers who did not care about American politics. The young people

"I doth detest these clickbaiteth parchments."

"Clickbait" is a link you simply can't resist clicking because it's too enticing—but such links may lead to advertisements, propaganda, or malware.

running these sites would scrape news or "fake news" stories from US websites, usually right-wing ones because those tended to generate more clicks (and thus advertising revenue), and then write false and sensational clickbait headlines to generate large numbers of shares on Facebook.[1]

Spreaders of "fake news" can influence factor two perhaps even more easily. Fake news stories may already get a boost that will move them higher in algorithmically-sorted feeds thanks to users being caught by their clickbait headlines. But "fake news" stories can be more directly spread with the use of "bots" and "fake," or sock puppet, social media accounts.

A bot is a social media account that has been somehow automated to create or share posts. Sometimes bots on social media are benign—for example, there is a Twitter bot account called "Newfound Planets" that generates text hourly about whimsical and weird "newly discovered" planets.[2] These bots are often clearly labeled as bots in their names or account information, and simply exist as a fun and creative exercise.

Less ethical, if not downright malicious, are a particular type of bot sometimes called the "socialbot," which pretend to be actual human beings. There was a proliferation of these bots seen during the 2016 presidential election, but they have been around longer than that. Bot accounts may use stock photographs and made-up information to create their fake persona, but many steal pictures and other personal information from real users—including minors.[3] Social media marketing companies, among others, sell these bots to celebrities or others who want to inflate their follower accounts and get more likes and shares for their posts—which pushes them higher in the algorithmic feeds.[4]

And remember factor one of how news spreads—who your friends are? Bots are invading your friends list, too. Researchers at the University of British Columbia, Vancouver examined how bots sent out friend requests to random Facebook users, then targeting "mutuals" over the next six weeks to infiltrate the social network and gain access to personal data.[5] In 2017, it was estimated that up to 15 percent of Twitter accounts (~48 million) were bots[6] and Facebook admitted that 2–3 percent of its 2.1 billion accounts (~63 million) were bots, with an additional 6–10 percent of accounts (~210 million) being duplicates.[7] Do you know all of your social media friends and followers personally? If not, some of them might very well be bots.

Social media bots can be packaged into groups that will act in concert to like, post, and share posts together. These are called botnets. Botnets have been used to amplify hate speech, abuse, and "fake news" stories. Botnets manipulate the social media sites' algorithms to make certain that their stories or viewpoints are prioritized in feeds, and spread. Use of botnets was observed starting in 2016 to support Donald Trump, Brexit, far-right candidate Marine Le Pen in France, and the far-right Alternative for Germany Party in their respective elections. Per Ben Nimmo, information defense fellow for the Atlantic Council (a non-profit, nonpartisan international affairs think tank), "A group of maybe a dozen people can create the impression of anything between 20,000 and 40,000 tweets in an hour. They can then push that hashtag into the trending lists."[8]

Research by Shao et al. at Indiana University has shown that, "Accounts that actively spread misinformation are significantly more likely to be bots... Social bots play a key role in the spread of fake news." Once the "fake news" has been given an algorithmic boost by the bots, humans can be fooled into continuing the spread—though some human users deliberately spread false information as well.[9] A study by Guess, Nyhan, and Reifler of the 2016 election proliferation of "fake news" found that one in four Americans had visited a "fake news" site between October 7 and November 14, 2016. "Fake news" was most driven by Facebook—and viewed most often by a small set of "hyper-political older conservatives" whose opinions likely were bolstered and strengthened by what they saw[10, 11]—it fed directly to their confirmation bias. Even if there's a particular group that's more likely to fall victim to fake news, it's important to not let that fact feed into your own bias toward yourself and lead you to believe you are immune.

All of these manipulations by bots and the creators of "fake news" are aimed directly at the confirmation bias of social media users. Real users see fake stories that play to their biases and pass them along. Spreaders of "fake news" get advertising clicks from people who want to believe their fantastic and malicious stories are true—and manipulate their opinions to become even more polarized. Once that damage has been done, it's extremely difficult to undo.

Corrections, Debunking, and the Backfire Effect

Sometimes news articles contain incorrect information; when this happens, the publisher will often correct the article.

Fake news stories are typically aimed directly at the confirmation bias of social media users. Real users see fake stories that play to their biases and pass them along.

Corrections may be issued in a separate column (common in print media), or an online article may be edited to reflect the corrections with the time and content of the edits noted. There's always a question of whether or not the correction will be as popular as the original article, particularly as news articles spread virally across social media.

Almost as long as "fake news" or false claims have existed, there have been people who seek to "debunk" them, exposing their falsehoods and misrepresentations. Corrections and

How to Spot a Bot

Ben Nimmo of the Atlantic Council summarizes bot-spotting with three As:[12]

Activity: Bot accounts push out a lot of posts in a very short amount of time. Look at how old the account is versus how many tweets or posts it has. If the answer is more than fifty to one hundred posts per day, be suspicious.

Anonymity: The less personal information, the more likely the account is to be a bot. Is the bio nothing but a political statement and the picture a random cartoon? Some bots do steal the personal information of real people, including pictures; a reverse image search is also useful.

Amplification: Does the account mostly just repost other content? Does it make the same post verbatim over and over again? Is it a low activity account with an enormous number of shares on its few posts?

debunking are the best and sometimes only tools at hand to fight the spread of false information, and yet they often either do not work or have the opposite effect. When a false belief is strengthened after being confronted with contrary evidence or a thorough debunking, this is called the backfire effect. It may seem unbelievable that someone, presented with evidence that they've been wrong, would instead double down—but it's an effect related to confirmation bias.

Some of this persistence of beliefs was seen in the 1970s Stanford experiments we talked about earlier in this book.[13, 14] When students were told that their rate of identification of suicide notes was wrong, or that the firefighter profiles they read were fake, the conclusions they drew didn't change. A 2010 study by Nyhan and Reifler found that when corrections were presented for the political misperceptions of people, minds were rarely changed and there were several instances of the backfire effect where subjects became even more convinced.[15]

Two years later, Nyhan and Reifler et al. examined the myth that President Obama was Muslim and found limited success in terms of how the correction was phrased—"I am a Christian, Obama says," was more successful than "I am not a Muslim, Obama says." They also found that self-identified Republicans were most resistant to these corrections, and there was a significant effect on if the researchers visibly involved were white or non-white.[16] The phrasing relates to the ease with which subjects could interpret the statements to agree with their confirmation bias, and the apparent race of the experimenters showed an influence of "social desirability"—subjects were

How can you fight fake news? Corrections and debunking often have the opposite effect on fake news because confirmation bias is so strong. Sometimes people only become more convinced that the myth is indeed fact.

perhaps more conscious of not wanting to appear racist in front of non-white researchers.

A 2014 study that Nyhan and Reifler did examined how people who held anti-vaccination beliefs would react to having their misperceptions about the flu vaccine challenged. They provided one group in their experiment with a correction to the common misunderstanding that the flu vaccine can cause the flu. After this debunking, some subjects still clung to their false beliefs, as we might now expect. But stranger, some of the group who had been most "concerned" about the flu vaccine accepted the debunking but said that they were even less willing to be vaccinated in light of that knowledge.[17]

Even more frustrating for people with an interest in spreading the truth, debunking false stories can make them even more popular. Beyond those doubling down thanks to the confirmation bias-fueled backfire effect, a 2005 *Journal of Consumer Research* study found other people tend to "misremember" the debunking as a positive endorsement of the false story itself.[18] This might play into another confirmation bias effect—biased memory.

Correcting falsehoods as they spread across social media isn't an entirely hopeless and thankless task, however. In a 2010 paper by Redlawsk et al., the researchers noted, "We show experimental evidence that such an effective tipping point does in fact exist."[19] This means there is some facts that will eventually convince most people to abandon their "motivated reasoning."

When Social Media and the Real World Collide

Having false beliefs fed and strengthened on social media impairs our decision-making as individuals and as a society. There are important issues that face all people of the world, like global climate change; and social media-fed confirmation bias hurts our ability to even discuss solutions. But there are even more specific ways that confirmation bias, grown and fed on social media, reaches into the real world and harms people. Let's look at a few examples of how social media and the real world collide.

Pizzagate and Comet Ping Pong

One of the most recent and frightening examples of social media reaching out into the real world is the so-called Pizzagate conspiracy theory, which ultimately led to a man armed with an AR-15, a revolver, and a knife walking into a popular restaurant in Washington, DC, on December 4, 2016, and firing three shots. Thankfully, no one was injured.[1]

Comet Ping Pong was caught in the middle of fake news, conspiracy theories, and confirmation bias when a man came into the popular restaurant with a gun, convinced the owner was operating a child slave ring.

Pizzagate started as a fringe conspiracy theory created by white supremacists and right-wing message board users, and it spread quickly through social media. At their most basic, conspiracy theories are products of confirmation bias, twisting causes of real events in a way that affirms the worldview of those who spread them.[2] It's impossible to know how much of Pizzagate was created by "honest" conspiracy theorists and how much of it was a cynical attempt to attack and hurt Hillary Clinton—who had already lost the election by the time Pizzagate hit its peak. But it does show how easy it is for social media to be manipulated by people motivated to spread a false story. While it's also impossible to know how many real people (as opposed to bots) genuinely believed the conspiracy, it only takes one person, exposed to the story at the wrong time, to bring the social media hysteria into reality in the worst possible way.

In late October/early November of 2016, a white supremacist Twitter account falsely claimed that there was evidence in emails taken from disgraced former Democratic congressman Anthony Weiner that Hillary Clinton was involved in an "international child enslavement ring."[3]

With the 2016 presidential election reaching a fever pitch, the claim spread virally across social media. Conspiracy theorists on various message boards such as 4chan spread the claim that Clinton was linked to a "pedophile sex ring" according to "FBI sources." These conspiracy claims were picked up by right-wing "fake news" sites, some of them out of Macedonia, and spread more quickly. The "fake news" sites and right-wing bot accounts began echoing the stories back and forth.

Conspiracy theorists picked through the Democratic emails hacked by Russians and released to WikiLeaks, particularly those of the chair of the Clinton campaign, John Podesta, looking for more "evidence." In the Podesta emails, Comet Ping Pong, a popular restaurant whose owner does have ties to powerful Democrats, was mentioned several times, generally to do with ordering food for volunteers or events. The conspiracy theorist and troll social media accounts "interpreted" code words from these emails. For example, one claim was that the oft-mentioned "cheese pizza" at Comet Ping Pong meant "child pornography."[4]

The conspiracy theorists became fixated on Comet Ping Pong and spread even more false allegations about the restaurant and its owner, fueled by bots and fake news sites such as Infowars—and by retweets from Donald Trump himself. Employees of the restaurant were targeted and harassed. Comet Ping Pong was bombarded with as many as 150 threatening phone calls a day.[5, 6, 7]

On November 7, a navy reserve officer named Posobiec saw the social media buzz and decided to investigate Comet Ping Pong himself. He and a friend went to the restaurant and began to broadcast video from it using Periscope. When he tried to take his phone, recording video, into a back room where a child was having a birthday party, the management asked him to leave. Management thought it was highly inappropriate for a stranger to record and broadcast the activities of children at their restaurant. Posobiec's video seemed to only add more fuel to the fire, with the #Pizzagate hashtag appearing on Twitter and being pushed heavily by bots. Conspiracy theorists demanded to know what management was hiding by not wanting Posobiec to film the children. Harassment of the restaurant and its employees continued unabated.

Less than a month later, on December 4, Edgar Welch walked into the restaurant with his AR-15 and revolver. The police were eventually able to talk the suspect down, and he was taken into custody with no one injured. When asked why he had done it, Welch stated, that he "had read online that the Comet restaurant was harboring child sex slaves" and that he "wanted to see for himself if they were there."[8]

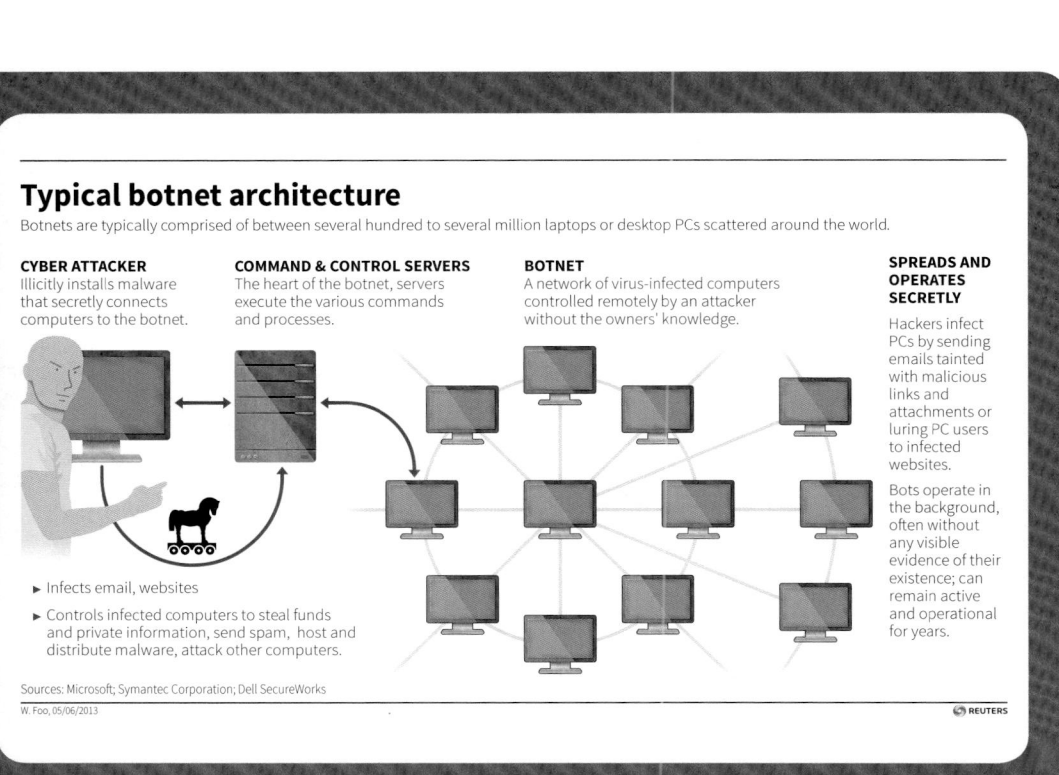

Typical botnet architecture

Botnets are typically comprised of between several hundred to several million laptops or desktop PCs scattered around the world.

CYBER ATTACKER
Illicitly installs malware that secretly connects computers to the botnet.

COMMAND & CONTROL SERVERS
The heart of the botnet, servers execute the various commands and processes.

BOTNET
A network of virus-infected computers controlled remotely by an attacker without the owners' knowledge.

SPREADS AND OPERATES SECRETLY
Hackers infect PCs by sending emails tainted with malicious links and attachments or luring PC users to infected websites.

Bots operate in the background, often without any visible evidence of their existence; can remain active and operational for years.

▶ Infects email, websites

▶ Controls infected computers to steal funds and private information, send spam, host and distribute malware, attack other computers.

Sources: Microsoft; Symantec Corporation; Dell SecureWorks

W. Foo, 05/06/2013

REUTERS

Pizzagate and other conspiracies are often pushed by botnets, which can operate faster than a single group of people posting. Botnets allow fake news to flourish.

Within hours, the same people who had pushed the Pizzagate conspiracy theory decided that the arrest was a "false flag"—a government plant to discredit their conspiracy.[9]

Posobiec and Welch were both men inclined to believe at least some of the claims of Pizzagate because of their internal biases. Posobiec, a self-described "Republican political operative," said that the Clinton campaign was "full of secrecy and deception."[10] Welch was someone already inclined to believe in conspiracy theories (such as 9/11 trutherism) and viewed himself as a hero who could save the children being threatened by the made-up trafficking ring.[11] Pizzagate fed and confirmed their worldviews in the darkest way possible.

Pizzagate is a uniquely modern phenomenon of social media and sets the blueprint for "fake news" conspiracy theory pushing in the future. There have always been conspiracy theories, but social media allowed this one to propagate in record time, using algorithmic manipulation by bots. The "#Pizzagate" hashtag on Twitter was pushed by bots and botnets, particularly those based out of the Czech Republic, Cyprus, and Vietnam. The conspiracy theory was featured prominently on "fake news" sites and the stories about it amplified by bots, even as it was discussed and amped up by users on 4chan and Reddit.[12]

Juries and Social Media

In our justice system (and others around the world that use juries), jurors are only supposed to consider the evidence that has been presented to them in court.

This allows juries to ideally be impartial and fair. There are strict rules in court about what can and cannot be presented, about keeping certain aspects of crimes or the history of the accused secret so that a jury's perceptions aren't tainted. This was already a difficult task in the days of newspapers and television news—and now we're in the age of social media.

Jury verdicts have been thrown out multiple times because of the social media activity of jurors. For example, in 2010, a verdict was overturned because one of the jurors called the defendant guilty on Facebook before the trial had finished.[13]

Juries are supposed to be impartial and fair, but the internet makes that more difficult every day, given the social media activity and consumption of jurors.

Highly public cases, like that of George Zimmerman in the 2012 fatal shooting of Trayvon Martin, bring out a lot of discussion on social media—not all of it truthful. There have also been concerns about public figures using their voice on social media to influence potential jurors, thus making the work of prosecutors more difficult. For example, President Trump has tweeted about how certain defendants should receive the death penalty. According to Rob Owen, a Northwestern University

How to Fight Confirmation Bias

The first step to combating confirmation bias is acknowledging that we can make mistakes and come to incorrect conclusions. Being open to information that disagrees with your beliefs, considering its worth, and deciding if it warrants changing what you think is the best armor you have. Here are other ways to fight the echo chamber:

Cast a wide net when you do research—don't just search for sources that agree with the conclusion you already have.

Confirm social media stories on reputable fact-checking sites. Snopes.com focuses on rumors and conspiracy theories. Politifact.com focuses on political stories.

Be aware of sources. Did the article come from a "fake news" site? Mainstream news sites also have political biases that you can look up.

Look for other viewpoints and listen to them.

Consider what it would take to prove your belief wrong—and if it's reasonable.

law professor and former assistant federal public defender, "The more publicity the president's comments receive, the more difficult it may eventually be to seat an unbiased jury… because jurors might be influenced by having heard that the president has demanded a particular outcome in the case."[14]

We've already talked about the spread of misinformation in the social media echo chamber, and the way people latch on to things that confirm what they already believe. Social media is a gateway for jurors to receive "prejudicial communication" — read opinions that will confirm their biases about a defendant one way or the other and make a fair trial impossible.

Think About What You Know

Confirmation bias is a quirk of human thought that has always been with us. Maybe one day, far in the future, we will have evolved past it. But until then, the best way to keep our thinking clear and our heads grounded in reality as much as possible is to always beware when someone or something is telling us exactly what we want to hear—and to be vigilant on social media.

CHAPTER NOTES

Introduction

1. Phil Plait, *Bad Astronomy: Misconceptions and Misuses Revealed, from Astrology to the Moon Landing "Hoax"* (New York, NY: John Wily & Sons, 2002).
2. "Vaccines Do Not Cause Autism," CDC.gov. https://www.cdc.gov/vaccinesafety/concerns/autism.html.
3. "In an Age of 'Alternative Facts,' a Massacre of Schoolchildren is Called a Hoax," *LA Times*, February 3, 2017, http://www.latimes.com/nation/la-na-sandy-hook-conspiracy-20170203-story.html.
4. "Climate Change Skepticism May Hinge on Personal Experience," BU.edu, https://www.bu.edu/research/articles/climate-change-skepticism/.

Chapter 1
A Brief History of Confirmation Bias

1. Thucydides, translated by Thomas Hobbes, History of the Peloponnesian War, perseus.tufts.edu, http://www.perseus.tufts.edu/hopper/text?doc=Thuc.%2B1.1.1&redirect=true.
2. Ibn Khaldû , translated by Rosenthal, Franz, *The Muqadimmah*(Princeton, NJ: Princeton University Press, 1967).

3. Leo Tolstoy, translated by Garnett, Constance, *The Kingdom of God Is Within You*, Project Gutenberg, 2002.

4. P. C. Wason, "Reasoning." In B. Foss (Ed.), *New Horizons in Psychology* (Harmondsworth: Penguin Books, 1966), pp. 135–151.

5. P. C. Wason, "Reasoning about a rule," *Quarterly Journal of Experimental Psychology*, 20, (1968), pp. 273–281.

6. P. C. Wason, "Structural simplicity and psychological complexity: Some thoughts on a novel problem," *Bulletin of the British Psychological Society*, 22, (1969a), pp. 281–284.

7. P. C. Wason, "Regression in reasoning?" *British Journal of Psychology*, 60, (1969b), pp. 471–480.

8. Joshua Klayman and Young-Won Ha, "Confirmation, Disconfirmation and Information in Hypothesis Testing," *Psychological Review*, 94, (1987), pp. 211–22.

9. C. Lord, L. Ross, and M. Lepper, "Biased Assimilation and Attitude Polarization: The Effects of Prior Theories on Subsequently Considered Evidence," *JPSP*, 37, (1979), pp. 2098–2109.

10. L. Ross, M.R. Lepper, and M. Hubbard, "Perseverance in Self-Perception and Social Perception: Biased Attributional Processes in the Debriefing Paradigm," *Journal of Personality and Social Psychology*, 32, (1975), pp. 880–892.

11. Tobias Greitemeyer, "I Am Right, You Are Wrong: How Biased Assimilation Increases the Perceived Gap Between Believers and Skeptics of Violent Video Game Effects," *PLOS One* (2014).

Chapter 2

Social Media Algorithms and Confirmation Bias

1. "You Actually Don't Mind Instagram Messing Your Timeline," Engadget, August 8, 2017, https://www.engadget.com/2017/08/08/instagram-algorithm/.
2. Ibid.
3. "Snapchat Starts Algorithm-Personalized Redesign Splitting Social and Media," TechCrunch, November 29, 2017, https://techcrunch.com/2017/11/29/snapchat-redesign/.
4. "Algorithmic Feeds Force Us to Compete," TechCrunch, March 19, 2016, https://techcrunch.com/2016/03/19/welcome-to-the-social-colosseum/.
5. Paul Covington, Jay Adams, and Emre Sargin, "Deep Neural Networks for YouTube Recommendations," *Proceedings of the 10th ACM Conference on Recommender Systems* (2016).
6. "'Fiction is outperforming reality': How YouTube's Algorithm Distorts Truth," *The Guardian*, February 2, 2018, https://www.theguardian.com/technology/2018/feb/02/how-youtubes-algorithm-distorts-truth.
7. "Who Controls Your Facebook Feed," Slate, January 3, 2016, http://www.slate.com/articles/technology/cover_story/2016/01/how_facebook_s_news_feed_algorithm_works.html.
8. "Twitter's New Order," Slate, March 5, 2017, http://www.slate.com/articles/technology/cover_story/2017/03/twitter_s_timeline_algorithm_and_its_effect_on_us_explained.html.
9. Ibid.

10. "Rise of the Racist Robots–How AI is Learning All Our Worst Impulses," *The Guardian*, August 8, 2017, https://www. theguardian.com/inequality/2017/aug/08/rise-of-the-racist-robots-how-ai-is-learning-all-our-worst-impulses.

11. "Machine Bias," Pro Publica, March 23, 2016, https:// www.propublica.org/article/machine-bias-risk-assessments-in-criminal-sentencing.

12. Michela Del Vicario, et al., "The Spreading of Misinformation Online," *Proceedings of the National Academy of Sciences of the United States of America*, 113, (2016), pp. 554–559.

13. "The Secret Psychology of Facebook: Why We Like, Share, Comment, and Keep Coming Back," bufferapp.com, https:// blog.bufferapp.com/psychology-of-facebook.

14. Ibid.

Chapter 3

Creating Your Own Bias Bubble

1. "Filter Bubbles Are a Serious Problem with News, Says Bill Gates," Quartz, February 21, 2017, https://qz.com/913114/bill-gates-says-filter-bubbles-are-a-serious-problem-with-news/.

2. "13 Reasons to Mute People on Twitter," *The Guardian*, May 13, 2014, https://www.theguardian.com/technology/2014/may/13/twitter-mute-unfollow-block-reason-secret-abuse.

3. "'A Honeypot for Assholes': Inside Twitter's 10-Year Failure to Stop Harassment," BuzzFeed News, August 11, 2016, https:// www.buzzfeed.com/charliewarzel/a-honeypot-for-assholes-inside-twitters-10-year-failure-to-s?utm_term=.bcXONRqEQp#. qhz8J4RjwM.

4. "How to Fix Facebook—Before It Fixes Us," Washington Monthly, https://washingtonmonthly.com/magazine/january-february-march-2018/how-to-fix-facebook-before-it-fixes-us/.
5. "Political Polarization and Media Habits," Pew Research Center Journalism & Media, October 21, 2014, http://www.journalism.org/2014/10/21/political-polarization-media-habits/#social-media-conservatives-more-likely-to-have-like-minded-friends.
6. "How Does Facebook Suggest Groups For me to Join?," facebook.com, https://www.facebook.com/help/382485908586472?helpref=uf_permalink.
7. "About Twitter's Account Suggestions," twitter.com, https://help.twitter.com/en/using-twitter/account-suggestions.
8. "How Does Instagram Suggest Friends?," Women.com, December 6, 2017, https://www.women.com/connieliou/lists/how-does-instagram-suggest-friends.
9. "The Cambridge Analytica Files," The Guardian, March 17, 2018, https://www.theguardian.com/news/2018/mar/17/data-war-whistleblower-christopher-wylie-faceook-nix-bannon-trump.
10. "How Researchers Leaned to Use Facebook 'Likes' to Sway Your Thinking," The New York Times, March 20, 2018, https://www.nytimes.com/2018/03/20/technology/facebook-cambridge-behavior-model.html.
11. "How Cambridge Analytica Turned Facebook 'Likes' into a Lucrative Political Tool," The Guardian, March 17, 2018, https://www.theguardian.com/technology/2018/mar/17/facebook-cambridge-analytica-kogan-data-algorithm.
12. "Cambridge Analytica Execs Boast of Role in Getting Donald Trump Elected," The Guardian, March 20, 2018, https://

www.theguardian.com/uk-news/2018/mar/20/cambridge-analytica-execs-boast-of-role-in-getting-trump-elected.

13. "Data Firm Says 'Secret Sauce' Aided Trump; Many Scoff," *The New York Times*, March 6, 2018, https://www.nytimes.com/2017/03/06/us/politics/cambridge-analytica.html.

Chapter 4
News, "Fake News," and Confirmation Bias

1. "News Use Across Social Media Platforms 2017," Pew Research Center Journalism & Media, September 7, 2017, http://www.journalism.org/2017/09/07/news-use-across-social-media-platforms-2017/.

2. "Sean Hannity Rips CNN's 'Alt-Left' Brian Stelter as 'Purveyor of Fake News,'" The Wrap, December 7, 2016, https://www.thewrap.com/sean-hannity-fox-news-cnn-brian-stelter-fake-news-donald-trump/.

3. "The Real Story of 'Fake News,'" merriam-webster.com, https://www.merriam-webster.com/words-at-play/the-real-story-of-fake-news.

4. Willian Weir, *History's Greatest Lies: the Startling Truths Behind World Events Our History Books Got Wrong* (Beverly, Massachusetts: Fair Winds Press, 2009).

5. Daniel Khaneman, *Thinking, Fast and Slow* (New York, NY: Farrar, Straus and Giroux, 2011).

6. "People Choose News That Fits Their Views," Live Science, June 7, 2009, https://www.livescience.com/3640-people-choose-news-fits-views.html.

7. Eytan Bakshy, Solomon Messing, and Lada A. Adamic, "Exposure to Ideologically Diverse News and Opinion on Facebook," *Science*, 6239, (2015), pp. 1130–1132.

8. "Democrats and Republicans Both Adept at Ignoring Facts Study Finds," Live Science, January 24, 2006, https://www.livescience.com/576-democrats-republicans-adept-ignoring-facts-study-finds.html.

9. "Blame the Echo Chamber on Facebook. But Blame Yourself, Too," Wired, November 25, 2016, https://www.wired.com/2016/11/facebook-echo-chamber/.

10. "Fake News: How Going Viral Feeds the Murky Monster of Truth," *The Independent UK*, January 24, 2018, http://www.independent.co.uk/news/long_reads/fake-news-viral-trump-jeremy-corbyn-traingate-twitter-agenda-truth-a8173951.html.

11. Stefan Stieglitz, Stefan and Linh Sang-Xuan, "Emotions and Information Diffusion in Social Media — Sentiment of Microblogs and Sharing Behavior," *Journal of Management Information Systems*, vol. 29 issue 4, (2014), pp. 217–248.

12. "What Facebook Did to American Democracy," *The Atlantic*, October 12, 2017, https://www.theatlantic.com/technology/archive/2017/10/what-facebook-did/542502/.

13. "The Data That Turned the World Upside Down," Motherboard, January 28, 2017, https://motherboard.vice.com/en_us/article/mg9vvn/how-our-likes-helped-trump-win.

14. "Did Russia Affect the 2016 Election? It's Now Undeniable," Wired, February 16, 2018, https://www.wired.com/story/did-russia-affect-the-2016-election-its-now-undeniable/.

15. Sir Arthur Conan Doyle. *The Coming of the Fairies* (Project Gutenberg, 2014).

16. Paul Smith, "The Cottingley Fairies: The End of a Legend," in Peter Narváez, *The Good People: New Fairylore Essays* (Lexington, KY: The University Press of Kentucky, 1991).

17. "Reporter Confirmation Bias Leads to Spread of Fake Negative News About Donald Trump," *The Washington Times*, February 2, 2017, https://www.washingtontimes.com/news/2017/feb/2/reporter-confirmation-bias-leads-spread-fake-news/.

18. Joshua Kalla and David E. Broockman, "The Minimal Persuasive Effects of Campaign Contact in General Elections: Evidence From 49 Field Experiments," *American Political Science Review* (2017).

19. "How Much Did Russian Interference Affect the 2016 Election?," FiveThirtyEight, February 16, 2018, https://fivethirtyeight.com/features/how-much-did-russian-interference-affect-the-2016-election/.

20. "This is How Facebook's Fake-news Writers Make Money," *The Washington Post*, November 18, 2016, https://www.washingtonpost.com/news/the-intersect/wp/2016/11/18/this-is-how-the-internets-fake-news-writers-make-money/?utm_term=.3307e5223f90.

21. "Scheme Created Fake News Stories to Manipulate Stock Prices, SEC Alleges," *LA Times*, July 5, 2017, http://www.latimes.com/business/la-fi-sec-fake-news-20170705-story.html.

22. "The (Almost) Complete History of 'Fake News'," BBC News, January 22, 2018, http://www.bbc.com/news/blogs-trending-42724320.

Chapter 5
The Spread of "Fake News" on Social Media

1. "How Teens in the Balkans Are Duping Trump Supporters With Fake News," BuzzFeed News, November 3, 2016, https://www.buzzfeed.com/craigsilverman/how-macedonia-became-

a-global-hub-for-pro-trump-misinfo?utm_term=.it1z6Wm9M7#.
yyB645kDx8.

2. "My Favorite Twitter Account is a Bot," Mashable, December
30, 2017, https://mashable.com/2017/12/30/my-favorite-
twitter-user-is-a-bot/#QFeJx6DEdOqs.

3. "The Follower Factory," *The New York Times*, January 27,
2018, https://www.nytimes.com/interactive/2018/01/27/
technology/social-media-bots.html.

4. "Twitter Bots Are Stealing Social Media Identities for Profit,"
NBC News, January 29, 2018, https://www.nbcnews.
com/tech/social-media/twitter-bots-are-stealing-social-media-
identities-profit-n841951.

5. Yazan Boshmaf, et al., "The Socialbot Network: When Bots
Socialize for Fame and Money," *Proceedings of the 27th Annual
Computer Security Applications Conference* (2011).

6. "As Many as 48 Million Twitter Accounts Aren't People,
Says Study," CNBC, March 10, 2017, https://www.cnbc.
com/2017/03/10/nearly-48-million-twitter-accounts-could-
be-bots-says-study.html.

7. "Facebook Quietly Admits to as Many as 270 Million Fake
or Clone Accounts," Mashable, November 2, 2017, https://
mashable.com/2017/11/02/facebook-phony-accounts-
admission/#B7x2eNjSsPq0.

8. "Troll Factories, Bots and Fake News: Inside the Wild West of
Social Media," Al Jazeera, February 7, 2018, http://www.
aljazeera.com/blogs/americas/2018/02/troll-factories-bots-
fake-news-wild-west-social-media-180207061815575.html.

9. Chengcheng Shao, et al., "The Spread of Misinformation by
Social Bots," Cornell University Library (2017).

10. "'Fake News' Went Viral in 2016. This Expert Studied Who Clicked," NBC News, January 14, 2018, https://www.nbcnews.com/politics/politics-news/fake-news-went-viral-2016-expert-studied-who-clicked-n836581.

11. Andrew Guess, Brendan Hyhan, and Jason Reifler, "Selective Exposure to Misinformation: Evidence From the Consumption of Fake News During the 2016 U.S. Presidential Campaign," Dartmouth College (2018).

12. Ibid.

13. Ibid.

14. Ibid.

15. Brendan Nyhan, and Jason Reifler, "When Corrections Fail: The Persistence of Political Misperceptions," *Political Behavior*, vol. 32 issue 2, (2010), pp. 303–330.

16. Brendan Nyhan, et al., "The Effect of Semantics and Social Desirability in Correcting the Obama Muslim Myth," *ResearchGate* (2012).

17. Brendan Nyhan, and Jason Reifler, "Does Correcting Myths About the Flu Vaccine Work? An Experimental Evaluation of the Effects of Corrective Information," *Vaccine*, vol. 33 issue 3, (2014), pp. 459–464.

18. Ian Skurnik, Carolyn Yoon, Denise C. Park, Norbert Schwarz, "How Warnings About False Claims Become Recommendations," *Journal of Consumer Research*, vol. 31 issue 4, (2005), pp. 713–724.

19. David P. Redlawsk, Andrew J. W. Civettini, Karen M. Emmerson, "The Affective Tipping Point: Do Motivated Reasoners Ever 'Get It'?", *Political Psychology*, vol. 31 issue 4, (2010), pp. 563–593.

Chapter 6
When Social Media and the Real World Collide

1. "Comet Pizza Gunman Pleads Guilty to Federal and Local Charges," *The Washington Post*, March 24, 2017, https://www.washingtonpost.com/local/public-safety/comet-pizza-gunman-to-appear-at-plea-deal-hearing-friday-morning/2017/03/23/e12c91ba-0986-11e7-b77c-0047d15a24e0_story.html?utm_term=.d8f4a85471be.

2. "Why Do Some People Believe in Conspiracy Theories?," *Scientific American*, https://www.scientificamerican.com/article/why-do-some-people-believe-in-conspiracy-theories/.

3. "How the Bizarre Conspiracy Theory Behind 'Pizzagate' Was Spread," BuzzFeed News, December 5, 2016, https://www.buzzfeed.com/craigsilverman/fever-swamp-election?utm_term=.jajGwRrOMX#.hclPAklnzo.

4. "How Pizzagate Went from Fake News to a Real Problem for a D.C. Business," PolitiFact, December 5, 2016, http://www.politifact.com/truth-o-meter/article/2016/dec/05/how-pizzagate-went-fake-news-real-problem-dc-busin/.

5. "Dissecting the #PizzaGate Conspiracy Theories," *The New York Times*, December 10, 2016, https://www.nytimes.com/interactive/2016/12/10/business/media/pizzagate.html.

6. "Pizzagate: From Rumor, to Hashtag, to Gunfire in D.C.," *The Washington Post*, December 6, 2016, https://www.washingtonpost.com/local/pizzagate-from-rumor-to-hashtag-to-gunfire-in-dc/2016/12/06/4c7def50-bbd4-11e6-94ac-3d324840106c_story.html?nid&utm_term=.882292ce7c56.

7. "Trump Retweets Right-Wing Provocateur Known for Pushing False Conspiracy Theories," *The Washington Post*, August

15, 2017, https://www.washingtonpost.com/news/morning-mix/wp/2017/08/15/trump-retweets-right-wing-provocateur-known-for-pushing-false-conspiracy-theories/?utm_term=.073c0c388b5e.

8. 'Pizzagate Conspiracy Gunman: 'I regret how I handled the situation,'" *The Guardian*, December 8, 2016, https://www.theguardian.com/us-news/2016/dec/08/pizzagate-conspiracy-gunman-i-regret-how-i-handled-the-situation.

9. Ibid.

10. Ibid.

11. Ibid.

12. Ibid.

13. "#Justice? Social Media's Impact on the US Jury System," American Bar Association, August 22, 2013, https://apps.americanbar.org/litigation/committees/trialevidence/articles/summer2013-0813-justice-social-media-impact-us-jury-system.html.

14. "Trump Tweets Could Sabotage Prosecutors in Truck Attack, Experts Say," NBC News, November 2, 2017, https://www.nbcnews.com/storyline/nyc-terrorist-attack/experts-trump-tweets-could-sabotage-prosecutors-truck-attack-n816946.

GLOSSARY

algorithm A set of rules, most often used by computers, that determine how a task will be accomplished.

backfire effect When a false belief is strengthened by being exposed to contrary evidence.

bot A social media account that has been somehow automated to create or share posts.

botnet A network of bots or socialbots that work together to amplify posts or hashtags.

clickbait Website content that's aimed at gaining "clicks" from users by means of emotionally manipulative, particularly sensationalist or outrageous, means.

confirmation bias The tendency of people to remember, seek out, and interpret information in such a way as to confirm beliefs they already have.

echo chamber An enclosed space that sound reverberates in; on social media, the enclosed social space where the only beliefs and opinions a user sees are those that echo their own.

fake news False news stories used to manipulate people or spread propaganda.

hyperbole   Deliberate, extreme overstatement, often for dramatic or manipulative effect.

post hoc rationalization   Rationalizing or coming up with logical explanations for an action after the fact.

prejudicial Something that causes harm or injury by promoting unfair bias.

proliferation   The act of increasing, but with a negative and dangerous connotation, such as "nuclear proliferation" meaning the increased manufacture of nuclear weapons.

proprietary   Something created exclusively by a company (or other owner of intellectual property rights) for its own use that is effectively a trade secret.

socialbot   A social media bot that purports to be an actual human being, while being an automated account.

sock puppet   A social media account that uses a pseudonym or other anonymizing profile information so that the real user is distanced from what the account does.

truism   A statement that is obviously true and implies nothing beyond what it states.

truther/trutherism   Originally a group of people who believe the US government was responsible for the September 11, 2001 attacks across the United States; later, someone who does not believe the accepted facts regarding an event and often favors a conspiracy theory instead.

FURTHER READING

Books

Brotherton, Rob. *Suspicious Minds: Why We Believe Conspiracy Theories.* New York, NY: Bloomsbury Sigma, 2017.

McRaney, David. *You Are Now Less Dumb: How to Conquer Mob Mentality, How to Buy Happiness, and All the Other Ways to Outsmart Yourself.* New York, NY: Avery, 2014.

Storr, Will. *The Unpersuadables: Adventures with the Enemies of Science.* New York, NY: Overlook Books, 2014.

Tavris, Carol, and Aronson, Elliot. *Mistakes Were Made (But Not by Me).* Wilmington, MA: Mariner Books, 2015

Websites

PolitiFact

www.politifact.com
A nonpartisan fact-checking site for political stories and claims.

Skeptical Science

www.skepticalscience.com
Dedicated to debunking arguments against global climate change, a topic hit hard by confirmation bias.

Snopes

www.snopes.com
Dedicated to debunking fake news stories, conspiracy theories, and rumors.

INDEX